Pressure Cookb

The Top Easy And Delicious Pressure Cooker Recipes!

Copyright ©

All rights reserved. No part of this book may be reproduced, stored in a retrieval system, or transmitted in any form or by any means, electronic, mechanical, photocopying, recording, scanning, or otherwise, without the prior written permission of the publisher.

Disclaimer

All the material contained in this book is provided for educational and informational purposes only. No responsibility can be taken for any results or outcomes resulting from the use of this material.

While every attempt has been made to provide information that is both accurate and effective, the author does not assume any responsibility for the accuracy or use/misuse of this information.

Table of Contents

Chapter 1: Pressure Cooker Soup And Stew Recipes 5

Pressure Cooker Chile Con Carne 6

Chickpea Soup 8

Barley Soup 10

Tomato Basil Soup 12

Vegetable Chicken Soup 14

Creamy Cauliflower Soup 16

Lentil Spinach Soup 18

Green Chile Chicken Chili 20

Potato And Bean Soup 22

Spicy Chicken Soup 23

Squash Soup 25

Tomato Chicken Rice Soup 27

Ham and Bean Stew 29

Mediterranean Turkey Soup 30

Chapter 2: Pressure Cooker Main Dish Recipes 32

Creamy Pressure Cooker Mushroom Chicken 33

Easy Pressure Cooker Butter Chicken 36

Beef Short Ribs 38

Honey Mustard Pork Chops 40

Chunky Beef Stew 42

Teriyaki Chicken 44

Juicy Pressure Cooker Pot Roast 45

Lemon Salmon 46

Garlic Honey Chicken 48

Lime Chicken Thighs 50

Chapter 1: Pressure Cooker Soup And Stew Recipes

Pressure Cooker Chile Con Carne

Ingredients

1 (2 1/2-pound) bottom round roast, trimmed and cut into 1-inch cubes

3/4 teaspoon salt, divided

2 medium onions, chopped

2 (6-inch) corn tortillas

4 teaspoons olive oil, divided

6 garlic cloves, minced

3 tablespoons chili powder

2 tablespoons ground ancho chile pepper

1 tablespoon ground cumin

3 tablespoons unsalted tomato paste

1 tablespoon finely chopped chipotle chile, canned in adobo sauce

1 teaspoon dried oregano

1 teaspoon lower-sodium soy sauce

1/4 teaspoon ground cinnamon

2 (14.5-ounce) cans unsalted fire-roasted diced tomatoes

1/2 ounce semisweet chocolate, chopped

Chopped green onions (optional)

1 sliced radish

1 tablespoon ground cumin

Directions

Place tortillas in the bowl of a food processor; process to form fine crumbs.

Heat a 6-quart pressure cooker over medium-high heat. Add 1 teaspoon oil to pan; swirl to coat. Sprinkle beef with 1/2 teaspoon salt. Add one-third of beef to pan; sauté 3 minutes or until browned on all sides. Remove beef from pan. Repeat procedure twice more with 1 teaspoon oil and one-third of beef.

Add remaining oil to pan; swirl to coat. Add onion and garlic; sauté 3 minutes. Add tortilla crumbs, chili powder, and next 8 ingredients; stir well. Stir in beef.

Close lid securely; bring to high pressure over high heat. Adjust heat to medium-high or level needed to maintain high pressure; cook 25 minutes. Remove from heat; let stand 20 minutes.

Place cooker under cold running water to release pressure. Remove lid; stir in chocolate and remaining salt, stirring until chocolate melts.

Top with green onions and radish, if desired.

Chickpea Soup

Ingredients

1 tablespoon olive oil

1 1/2 cups chopped onion

5 garlic cloves, minced

4 ounces Spanish chorizo, diced

2 1/2 cups water

2 1/2 cups fat-free, lower-sodium chicken broth

1 1/2 cups dried chickpeas (garbanzo beans)

2 bay leaves

6 cups chopped escarole

1 tablespoon sherry vinegar

3/8 teaspoon kosher salt

1/2 teaspoon freshly ground black pepper

1/4 teaspoon crushed red pepper

Directions

Heat a 6-quart pressure cooker over medium-high heat. Add oil to pan; swirl to coat. Add onion; sauté 3 minutes.

Add garlic and chorizo; sauté 2 minutes.

Stir in 2 1/2 cups water, broth, chickpeas, and bay leaves. Close lid securely; bring to high pressure over high heat.

Adjust heat to medium or level needed to maintain high pressure; cook 1 hour.

Remove from heat; release pressure through steam vent, or place cooker under cold running water to release pressure. Remove lid. Discard bay leaves.

Add escarole and remaining ingredients, stirring just until escarole wilts. Serve immediately.

Barley Soup

Ingredients

1 cup lentils, rinsed

2 stalks celery, sliced

½ cup hulled barley or ½ cup pearl barley

½ teaspoon oregano

6 cups water or 6 cups vegetable stock

½ teaspoon ground cumin

1 onion, chopped

¼ teaspoon black pepper

2 garlic cloves, minced or crushed

⅛-¼ teaspoon red pepper flakes

2 carrots, sliced

½ teaspoon salt (optional)

2 -4 cups fresh spinach (optional)

Directions

Put all ingredients except salt and spinach into cooker and bring it to high pressure.

Cook at high pressure for 12 minutes; then bring pressure down with a quick-release method. Lentils should be cooked, but barley may not be completely tender.

Cook until barley reaches the desired state of tenderness, about 15 minutes, adding water if a thinner consistency is needed. Then add salt and spinach, if desired.

Cook briefly until spinach is wilted but still bright green.

Tomato Basil Soup

Ingredients

2 (14.5 oz) cans chicken broth

3 lbs tomatoes – cored, peeled, and quartered

1/4 cup fresh basil

1 tablespoon tomato paste

1/2 teaspoon salt

1/2 teaspoon freshly ground black pepper

1/2 cup shredded Parmesan cheese

1 cup half and half

3 tablespoons butter

1 large onion, diced

2 stalks celery, diced

1 large carrot, diced

2 garlic cloves, minced or pressed

Directions

Melt butter in pressure cooker pot. Saute onions, celery, and carrots until tender. Add garlic and cook 1 minute stirring often. Add chicken stock, tomatoes, basil, tomato paste, salt, and pepper.

Select high pressure and 5 minutes cook time. When timer sounds turn pressure cooker off, wait 5 minutes and use Quick Pressure Release to release pressure.

When valve drops carefully remove lid. Puree mixture until it's very smooth.

Saute and stir in Parmesan and half and half.

Vegetable Chicken Soup

Ingredients

1 ½ lbs boneless skinless chicken breasts

1 onion, coarsely chopped

1 cup carrot, peeled and cut in 1 inch chunks

1 cup celery, cut in 1 inch chunks

¼ cup cilantro, chopped

½ cup green onion, chopped

3 garlic cloves, chopped

1 ½ teaspoons salt

½ teaspoon black pepper

4 cups water

1 ½ cups corn kernels, frozen

Directions

Cut chicken breasts into 1 inch cubes. Place chicken, onion, carrots, celery, cilantro, green onion, garlic, salt, pepper and water in pressure cooker.

Lock lid into place. Over high heat, bring cooker up to pressure. Then reduce heat to maintain pressure and pressure regulator rocks gently. Cook for 8 minutes.

Quickly release the pressure. Carefully remove lid and add frozen corn.

Heat on medium heat until corn is tender.

Creamy Cauliflower Soup

Ingredients

1 tablespoon coconut oil

1 white onion

3 cloves garlic

1 extra large or 2 medium sized fennel bulbs, stalks and fronds removed

1 pound cauliflower florets

1 cup coconut milk

3 cups broth (bone broth or vegetable broth)

2 teaspoons salt

Optional: Truffle oil, for serving

Optional: Black pepper for serving

Directions

Slice the onions, mince the garlic, and chop the fennel. If your cauliflower is not already chopped into florets, do that now.

In the bottom of your pressure cooker, heat up the coconut oil. Sauté the onions until translucent.

Add the garlic, fennel, and cauliflower. Sauté for 5-10 minutes, until the edges of the vegetables begin to turn golden.

Pour the broth and coconut milk into the pot. Add salt. Cook on the soup setting for at least 5 minutes.

Once the pressure cooker is done cooking, release the pressure and remove the lid.

Use a standing blender or an immersion blender to puree the soup to a smooth, creamy consistency.

Scoop into serving bowls and drizzle with truffle oil. Top with freshly cracker pepper, and garnish with a left over fennel frond. Serve hot.

Lentil Spinach Soup

Ingredients

4 cups chicken broth

4 cups water

1 1/2 cups brown lentils, rinsed

2 teaspoons cumin

1 teaspoon garlic salt

1/4 teaspoon red pepper flakes

2 tablespoons dried parsley

1/2 teaspoon salt

1/2 teaspoon pepper

1/2 cup orzo

2 cups roughly chopped baby spinach

1 tablespoon vegetable oil

1 onion, diced

3 carrots, diced

5 cloves garlic, minced

2 cans (15 oz.) diced tomatoes

Directions

Select sauté and add oil to cooking pot. When oil is hot, sauté onion and carrots until tender, about 8 minutes. Add garlic, cook for one minute. Add tomatoes, broth, water, lentils, cumin, garlic salt, red pepper flakes, parsley, salt and pepper.

Select high pressure and 10 minutes cook time. When beep sounds turn pressure cooker off, use a Quick Pressure Release to release the pressure.

When valve drops carefully remove lid, tilting away from you to allow steam to disperse.

Select Simmer and add orzo; simmer 10 minutes or until orzo and lentils are tender.

Add spinach and cook until spinach wilts.

Season to taste with additional salt and pepper if necessary.

Green Chile Chicken Chili

Ingredients

2 cans (14 ounce) chicken broth

1 jar (16 ounce) salsa verde

1 can (4 ounces) diced green chilies

1 teaspoon cumin

1/4 teaspoon red pepper flakes

2 cans (15.5 ounce) cannellini beans or other white bean, drained and rinsed

2 tablespoon cornstarch

3 tablespoon cold water

1 tablespoon vegetable oil

1 large onion, diced

2 cloves garlic, minced or pressed

3 cups cooked, diced or shredded chicken

Directions

Select Sauté and add the oil to the pressure cooker pot. When oil is hot, add the onion and cook, stirring occasionally until the onion is tender, about 5 minutes. Add the garlic and cook for an additional minute.

Add chicken, chicken broth, salsa verde, green chilies, cumin, red pepper flakes and beans to the pressure cooking pot. Lock lid in place, select High Pressure, 5 minutes cook time and press start.

When timer beeps, turn off pressure cooker, wait 5 minutes, then do a quick pressure release to release any remaining pressure.

In a small bowl, dissolve cornstarch in 3 tablespoons water. Select Simmer and add cornstarch mixture to the pot stirring constantly until chili thickens. Add salt and pepper to taste.

Served topped with sour cream, diced avocado, tortilla chips, and shredded cheese.

Potato And Bean Soup

Ingredients

2 lb potatoes, peeled and cut into chunks

1 lb leeks, trimmed and sliced into thin pieces

1 can cannellini beans, drained and rinsed

Marigold Swiss Bouillon Powder, as needed

Directions

Cook the potatoes in the pressure cooker with water to cover until just tender. Drain the cooking water into a bowl.

Reserve some of the potato pieces to add texture to the soup.

Measure the cooking water and make up the stock according to the guidelines on the carton. Puree the remaining potato and add the stock to it.

Meanwhile steam the leeks until cooked and add to the soup with the cooking liquid then add the beans and the reserved potato chunks.

Add freshly ground black pepper to taste. Serve hot with crusty bread.

Spicy Chicken Soup

Ingredients

2 (14.5 ounce) cans chicken broth

1/2 teaspoon salt

1 teaspoon ground black pepper

1 teaspoon garlic powder

2 tablespoons dried parsley

1 tablespoon onion powder

1 tablespoon chili powder

2 (16 ounce) cans black beans, drained

1 (15 ounce) bag frozen corn

2 tablespoons olive oil

1 large onion, diced

3 cloves garlic, minced or pressed

4 boneless, skinless chicken breasts

1 (16 ounce) jar mild chunky salsa

2 (14.5 ounce) cans peeled and diced tomatoes

Directions

Select Sauté and add olive oil to the pressure cooker pot. When oil is hot, add the onion and cook, stirring occasionally until the onion is tender, about 5 minutes. Add the garlic and cook for an additional minute.

Add remaining ingredients, except beans and corn. Lock lid in place, select High Pressure, 8 minutes cook time and press start.

When timer beeps, turn off pressure cooker, wait 10 minutes, then do a quick pressure release.

Remove chicken breasts from soup and dice or shred. Return chicken to soup and stir in black beans and corn.

If necessary, select Simmer and bring to a boil, stirring occasionally until beans and corn are heated.

Serve topped with shredded cheese, sour cream and tortilla strips, if desired.

Squash Soup

Ingredients
1 onion, diced

2 garlic cloves, minced

1 carrot, diced

2 stalks celery, diced

5 lbs butternut squash, cubed

4 cups chicken broth

2 tablespoons rosemary, fresh, chopped

1 teaspoon paprika

1 teaspoon nutmeg

salt and pepper

Directions
Sweat onion and garlic in small amount of oil in pressure cooker.

Add Carrot and Celery to color before adding all remaining ingredients.

Place Pressure cooker lid on and bring to pressure over medium heat. Once rocker begins to move at medium, to cook for twenty minutes. Remove from heat, allow to depressurize on countertop.

Using hand held blender, blend to smooth consistency, adding additional broth to thin, if needed.

Add additional salt and pepper, as needed.

Tomato Chicken Rice Soup

Ingredients

1 tablespoon olive oil

24 ounces boneless skinless chicken breasts

1 yellow onion, finely chopped

3 carrots, peeled and sliced 1/4 inch thick

3 garlic cloves, minced

1 teaspoon dried thyme

1 cup long grain rice

4 cups chicken stock

1 (28 ounce) can diced tomatoes

1 ½ teaspoons salt

1 teaspoon black pepper

¼ cup fresh parsley, chopped

2 celery ribs, sliced 1/4 inch thick

Directions

Pre-heat pressure cooker on the Brown setting. Dice chicken into bite-size pieces.

Add the olive oil to the pressure cooker and brown the chicken pieces briefly, seasoning with salt and pepper.

Add the onion, carrots, celery, garlic and thyme; saute for 2 to 3 minutes.

Stir in the rice, and pour in the stock and tomatoes. Season with salt and pepper to taste.

Lock lid in place, and cook on HIGH for 8 minutes.

Reduce the pressure with the quick-release method, and carefully remove the lid. Add the parsley, adjust seasoning if needed and serve.

Ham and Bean Stew

Ingredients

1 lb dried great northern beans

8 cups water

1 lb ham

2 teaspoons onion powder

½ teaspoon garlic powder

2 dried bay leaves

1 pinch crushed red pepper flakes

1 (10 ounce) package frozen chopped spinach

1 dash nutmeg

Fresh ground black pepper, to taste

Directions

Add washed, sorted dry beans to pressure cooker with the water.

Cut ham into small chunks and add all seasonings. Set to HIGH pressure for 20 - 25 minutes.

Use quick release method to release steam. Stir in spinach and nutmeg. Heat through and serve.

Mediterranean Turkey Soup

Ingredients

2 teaspoons olive oil

4 Italian turkey sausage links, casings removed

1 medium onion, diced

3 cloves garlic, minced

1/2 cup pearl barley

1 cup green lentils

1 bone-in chicken breast half, skin removed

1/2 cup chopped fresh parsley

3 cups chicken stock

1 (15 ounce) can chickpeas (garbanzo beans), drained

1 (16 ounce) bag fresh spinach leaves, chopped

1 cup mild salsa

Directions

Heat 1 teaspoon olive oil in a pressure cooker over medium heat. Add sausage meat, and cook until browned, breaking it into crumbles. Remove sausage to a plate and drain oil.

Add another 1 teaspoon of olive oil to pressure cooker; cook onion and garlic until onion is transparent.

Add barley and stir 1 minute. Return sausage to pressure cooker. Add lentils, chicken, parsley, and chicken stock to cooker, adding enough stock to completely cover chicken.

Close cover securely; place pressure regulator on vent pipe. Bring pressure cooker to full pressure over high heat.

Reduce heat to medium high; cook for 9 minutes. Pressure regulator should maintain a slow steady rocking motion; adjust heat if necessary.

Remove pressure cooker from heat; use quick-release following manufacturer's instructions or allow pressure to drop on its own.

Open cooker and remove chicken; shred meat and return to soup. Add garbanzo beans, spinach and salsa; stir to blend and heat through before serving.

Chapter 2: Pressure Cooker Main Dish Recipes

Creamy Pressure Cooker Mushroom Chicken

Ingredients

4-6 boneless, skinless chicken breast halves

16 oz fresh white button mushrooms, thinly sliced

1/4 cup evaporated milk

1/2 cup grated Parmesan cheese

2 tablespoon cornstarch

3 tablespoon cold water

2 tablespoon fresh parsley

1 teaspoon onion powder

1 teaspoon garlic powder

Salt and pepper to taste

2 tablespoon olive oil, divided

1 medium onion, minced

6 garlic cloves, minced

2 cups low sodium chicken broth

2 tablespoon white balsamic vinegar

1 tablespoon tomato paste

1 teaspoon dried thyme

Hot cooked rice

Directions

Season the chicken breasts on both sides with onion powder, garlic powder, salt and pepper to taste. Heat 1 tablespoon olive oil over medium heat in the pressure cooker.

Add the chicken in batches and brown lightly on both sides. Remove browned chicken from the pressure cooker; place on a plate. Heat the remaining 1 tablespoon olive oil in the pressure cooker over medium heat.

Add the onions and sauté for 2 minutes or until translucent. Add the garlic; cook and stir for 30 seconds. Stir in the chicken broth, vinegar, tomato paste and thyme. Place the rack in the pressure cooker; put the browned chicken on the rack. Add the sliced mushrooms.

Put the cover on the pressure and lock in place. Place the regulator on top if the pressure cooker uses one. When the pressure cooker reaches high pressure - 15 psi, set a timer and cook for 6 minutes.

Using the Quick Pressure Release method recommended for your pressure cooker, release pressure and remove the cover. Remove chicken and keep warm. Stir the evaporated milk, and Parmesan cheese into the sauce.

Combine the cornstarch and water, whisking until smooth. Stir the cornstarch mixture into the sauce and cook over medium/low heat, stirring constantly, until the sauce thickens. Stir in the chopped parsley.

Pour the sauce over the chicken and serve over rice.

Easy Pressure Cooker Butter Chicken

Ingredients

10 boneless skinless chicken thighs

2 tablespoons fresh ginger root, peeled and chopped

1/2 cup (1 stick) unsalted butter

2 teaspoons ground cumin

1 tablespoon paprika

2 teaspoons kosher salt

3/4 cup heavy cream

2 (14-oz) cans diced tomatoes and juice

2 jalapeno peppers, seeded and chopped

3/4 cup Greek yogurt

2 teaspoons garam masala

2 teaspoons ground roasted cumin seeds

2 tablespoons cornstarch

2 tablespoons water

1/4 cup firmly packed minced cilantro

Directions

Cut the chicken pieces into quarters.

Put tomatoes, jalapeno and ginger in a blender or food processor and blend to a fine puree.

Add butter to pressure cooking pot, select Browning. When butter is melted and foam begins to subside, add the chicken pieces, a few at a time, and sear until they are nicely browned all over for about 2-3 minutes per batch. Remove them with a slotted spoon into a bowl and put aside.

Add ground cumin and paprika to the butter in the pot and cook, stirring rapidly, for 10-15 seconds. Add the tomato mixture, salt, cream, yogurt and chicken pieces along with any juices that have accumulated in the bowl to the pot.

Gently stir the chicken to coat the pieces. Cover and lock lid in place. Select High Pressure and 5 minutes cook time. When timer beeps, turn off and use a natural pressure release for 10 minutes. After 10 minutes use a quick pressure release to release any remaining pressure.

Stir in the garam masala and roasted cumin. Whisk together cornstarch and water in a small bowl. Stir in to sauce in the pot. Select sauté and bring to a boil. Turn off pressure cooker and stir in minced cilantro.

Serve with rice.

Beef Short Ribs

Ingredients

4 large beef short ribs

2 tablespoons vegetable oil

2 slices bacon, finely chopped

1 large onion finely chopped

3 garlic cloves, minced or pressed

1/2 cup apple juice or dry red wine

1 cup beef both

2 tablespoons tomato paste

1 tablespoon cornstarch

1 tablespoon water

Directions

Season ribs generously with salt and pepper. Add oil to the pressure cooking pot, select Browning. When oil is hot, brown the ribs in small batches, do not overfill. Remove to a plate.

Add bacon to pressure cooking pot and cook until brown and crisp. Add onion to pressure cooking pot and sauté until tender for about 3 minutes. Add garlic and cook one minute more.

Add the apple juice and use a wooden spoon to scrape up any brown bits stuck on the bottom of the pot. Add beef broth, tomato paste, and ribs to pressure cooking pot, cover and lock lid in place. Select

High Pressure and 40 minutes cook time. When timer beeps do a natural pressure release for 10 minutes and then release any remaining pressure.

With tongs, remove ribs to a plate or bowl and cover with foil to keep warm. Use a fat scparator and a mesh strainer to separate the fat from the juices. Return juices to the cooking pot.

In a small bowl, combine cornstarch and water. Add to juices in the cooking pot. Select Sauté and bring to a boil, stirring constantly until juices thicken. Turn pressure cooker off.

Add ribs and stir to coat with the sauce. Put the lid back on the pressure cooker and allow the ribs to absorb some of the sauce for about 10 minutes stirring occasionally if sauce is still bubbling and serve.

Honey Mustard Pork Chops

Ingredients

4 medium cut Bone-in Pork Chops

½ cup onions, thinly sliced

3 tablespoons minced garlic

8 oz white button mushrooms, sliced

4 cups fresh green beans, chopped

2 cups chicken broth

3 Tablespoons cornstarch

¼ cup honey

½ cup dijon mustard

½ teaspoon salt

¼ teaspoon black pepper

1 tablespoon olive oil

Directions

Turn pressure cooker to sauté. Add olive oil and when pot is hot sear both sides of each pork chop. Remove seared pork chops from pot.

Pressure cooker still on sauté add, onions, and garlic, cook for 1-2 minutes. In a small bowl reserve ¼ cup of chicken broth and whisk in 2 Tablespoons cornstarch.

Pour remaining 1¾ cups of chicken broth into pressure cooker, slowly whisk in cornstarch mixture.

Stir in honey and mustard, salt and pepper. Add in the seared pork chops, mushrooms, and green beans in that order.

Lock lid and close pressure valve. Cook on High Pressure for 8-10 minutes.

Allow a 10-12 minute natural release. Remove green beans, mushrooms and pork chops from pressure cooker.

Turn Pressure Cooker back to sauté, whisk in remaining tablespoon of cornstarch to thicken sauce even more.

Chunky Beef Stew

Ingredients

1 1/2 lbs. beef stew meat

3 tbsp oil

1 can green beans with liquid

2 cans diced tomatoes with liquid

2 tbsp cornstarch

1/3 cup cold water

2 large potatoes

4-5 large carrots

1 large onion

Salt and pepper to taste

Directions

Cut the beef stew meat into bite size pieces. Do the same with the potatoes, carrots and onions.

Heat the pressure cooker over medium high heat. Add the oil and stew meat. Stir and cook until the meat is well browned all over. Add the potatoes, carrots, onion, beans with their liquid, and tomatoes with their liquid. Add salt and pepper to taste.

Place the lid and weight on the pressure cooker according to your manufacturer's instruction. Heat on medium high setting until pressure is achieved. Continue cooking for 15 minutes.

At the end of the 15 minutes cooking time, reduce the pressure immediately by running cold water on the top of the pressure cooker. When pressure releases, open the top of the cooker and place it back on the stove.

Combine the cornstarch and cold water in a small bowl. Bring the stew back up to the boil, add the cornstarch and water and stir until thickened and serve.

Teriyaki Chicken

Ingredients

1/4 cup low sodium soy sauce

3 tbsp rice wine

2 tbsp honey

2 cloves garlic

1 teaspoon fresh grated ginger

1 teaspoon siracha hot sauce

8 drumsticks (28 oz), skin removed

1 tbsp sesame seeds

Chopped scallions

Directions

Use saute button, when hot add soy sauce, rice wine, honey, garlic, ginger and sriracha and cook 2 minutes, stirring.

Add the chicken, cover and lock the lid. Cook on high pressure 15 to 20 minutes until the chicken is tender.

When pressure releases, finish with scallions and sesame seeds.

Juicy Pressure Cooker Pot Roast

Ingredients

3 1/2 lb beef chuck roast

1 tablespoon vegetable oil

1 large onion, roughly chopped

1 1/2 cup water or beef broth

2 bay leaves

Directions

Pat roast dry and season liberally with lemon pepper and seasonings of your choice.

Put oil in the cooking pot and select browning. When oil begins to sizzle, brown meat on both sides. Remove roast from the cooking pot and add onions, water and bay leaves. Put roast back in the cooking pot on top of the onions.

Select High Pressure. Set timer for 70 minutes. When timer sounds turn off pressure cooker and use a natural pressure release to release pressure for approximately 20 minutes. When valve drops carefully remove the lid.

Remove roast to a serving dish. Strain juices and discard onion and bay leaves. Thicken juices in cooking pot on simmer with some water and flour or cornstarch to make gravy.

Lemon Salmon

Ingredients

4 salmon fillets

2 tablespoons olive oil

1 teaspoon garlic, minced

2 anchovy fillets (optional) or 2 teaspoons anchove paste

1/2 teaspoon crushed red pepper

1 tablespoon butter

1 cup loosely pack parsley

juice and zest of 1 lemon

2 tablespoons capers

1 tablespoon olive oil

1 shallot, finely minced

1 cup long-grain rice

1 1/4 cups broth

1/4 cup lemon juice

1/2 cup white wine

1 teaspoon sea salt

1 tablespoon parsley, chopped

zest of 1 lemon

sea salt and ground pepper

lemon slices

Directions

Combine olive oil, garlic, anchovy (if using), crushed red pepper, and butter in a small saute pan over medium-high heat. Saute until the mixture is fragrant and garlic is golden, set aside.

To the bowl of a small food processor, add the parsley, juice and zest of 1 lemon, and capers. Spoon the olive oil and garlic mixture over top. Pulse until finely chopped. Scoop into a small bowl until ready to serve.

Add the olive oil and shallot to the pressure cooker. Saute until fragrant. Add rice. Cook 1-2 minutes. Add liquid, parsley, zest, salt and pepper.

Salt and pepper salmon portions on both sides. Place on steamer basket, and top with lemon slices. Set in the pressure cooker over the rice and liquid.

Lock pressure cooker. Set on rice setting, or about 4 minutes if using a stove top model. Remove from heat source if using a stove top model. Wait 5 minutes, then de-pressurize.

Lift steamer basket from pressure cooker. Fluff rice with a fork.

To serve, drizzle the Lemon Caper Chimichurri over the salmon and rice.

Garlic Honey Chicken

Ingredients

3 pounds boneless, skinless chicken thighs

1/2 teaspoon dried minced garlic

1 teaspoons Sriracha chili garlic sauce

3/4 cup soy sauce

3/4 cup ketchup

3/4 cup honey

2 tablespoons cornstarch

2 tablespoons water

1 tablespoon chopped fresh basil

Directions

Add garlic, chili sauce, soy sauce, ketchup and honey to pressure cooking pot. Stir to combine. Add chicken to the pot. Cover pot and lock lid in place.

Select High Pressure and 9 minutes cook time.

After cooking for 9 minutes, turn off pressure cooker and use a quick pressure release.

In a small bowl, dissolve cornstarch in 2 tablespoons water. Add cornstarch mixture to the sauce in the pot stirring constantly. Select

Simmer and bring to a boil, stirring constantly. After sauce thickens, add fresh basil to the sauce.

Lime Chicken Thighs

Ingredients

Juice and zest of 1 lime

3 garlic cloves, minced

1 teaspoon cumin

1 teaspoon chili powder

2 tablespoons olive oil divided

1/4 cup fresh cilantro, chopped

4 chicken thighs, about 1-1/2 pounds (I used bone in, skin on)

1/2 cup chicken stock

1 tablespoon arrowroot powder, tapioca starch or corn starch

Salt and pepper to taste

Directions

Place 1 tablespoon olive oil, lime juice, garlic, cumin, chili powder, cilantro and salt and pepper in a plastic ziploc or large glass dish and mix. Pat the chicken dry and add to the marinade. Allow to sit for at least 30 minutes, or up to 2 hours.

Set your pressure cooker to sauté and once hot, add the other tablespoon of olive oil. Remove the chicken from the marinade and add to the pot. Let it sear a few minutes on each side until it's golden. Then add 1/2 cup chicken stock, close the pot with the lid, and push the poultry button, and cook for 12 minutes..

Add the arrowroot powder to 2 tablespoons of cold water. Once the chicken is done, remove it from the pot, and hit sauté again. Add the arrowroot mixture.

Whisk the ingredients in the pan, making sure to pick up any fond from the chicken. Season as necessary. Once the sauce is thick and combined, turn the pot off.

Serve the chili lime chicken with sauce immediately.

Printed in Great Britain
by Amazon